55 Christmas Balls to Knit

Colourful Festive Ornaments · Tree Decorations
Centrepieces · Wreaths · Window Decorations

ARNE & CARLOS

Table of Contents

CHAPTER 1 :: PAGE 7
Introduction

CHAPTER 2 :: PAGE 10
Materials, Techniques, and Basic Instructions

CHAPTER 3 :: PAGE 33
It will be Christmas soon

CHAPTER 4 :: PAGE 41
Children's Mittens

CHAPTER 5 :: PAGE 47
Out on Your Skis, Life's Sure to Please

CHAPTER 6 :: PAGE 53
Tradition

CHAPTER 7 :: PAGE 57
A Ski Sweater

CHAPTER 8 :: PAGE 63
Christmas Greenery

CHAPTER 9 :: PAGE 69
December 23: Little Christmas Eve

CHAPTER 10 :: PAGE 77
The Night before Christmas

CHAPTER 11 :: PAGE 85
Christmas Goodies

CHAPTER 12 :: PAGE 91
Hearts

CHAPTER 13 :: PAGE 99
The Choir of Angels

CHAPTER 14 :: PAGE 103
Religious Motifs

CHAPTER 15 :: PAGE 111
Animals & Birds

CHAPTER 16 :: PAGE 121
Reindeer

CHAPTER 17 :: PAGE 129
Lights

CHAPTER 18 :: PAGE 135
A Christmas Journey

CHAPTER 19 :: PAGE 139
Conclusion – The Twelfth Day

First published in Great Britain in 2011 by Search Press Limited, Wellwood, North Farm Road, Tunbridge Wells, Kent TN2 3DR

Reprinted 2011, 2012, 2014, 2015

Also published in the United States of America in 2011 by Trafalgar Square Books North Pomfret, Vermont 05053

Originally published in Norwegian as Julekuler by Cappelen Damm A/S

© 2010 Cappelen Damm A/S
English translation © 2011 Trafalgar Square Books

ISBN: 978-1-84448-781-3

TRANSLATION BY CAROL HUEBSCHER RHOADES
ILLUSTRATIONS: ARNE & CARLOS
PHOTOGRAPHY: RAGNAR HARTVIG
STYLING: INGRID SKAANSAR
BOOK DESIGN: GINA ROSE

Printed in China with Oceanic Graphic Printing

10 9 8 7 6 5

We live *and work* in an old train station in a rural community in Etnedal, Valdres, Norway.

We have worked there as designers with our own fashion label since 2002. At first we managed the designs and production of both sewn and knitted garments that we sold to shops around the world. However, we always felt that the most inspiring aspect of our collections was the knitting. Our knitwear also got the best response from the buyers when we presented our collections at fashion shows abroad. It took a while before we realized it was clearly the knit designs we should focus on, and, five years after we launched our brand – Arne&Carlos – we finally decided to concentrate just on our knitwear designs. We completely changed our concepts and began to knit sweaters, jackets, and accessories such as scarves, hats, and mittens inspired by Nordic patterns and traditions.

We both grew up with knitting and crochet around us and perhaps because of that we find a special joy in working with knitting needles and yarn. After we discovered what we really wanted to do was right in front of our noses the whole time. We decided to take a step further and not only produce the finished garments but also develop patterns for hand knitting. And now we have finally published our first book of knitting patterns! Our method of designing involves assembling a mass of information and inspiration we then use to construct our own "universe" – and it is from this universe that all our designs emerge. Unfortunately we can't present very much of our inspirational sources or our universe along with the commercially-made knitwear we sell in shops. With this book we can finally show several aspects of our work – everything behind the designs and the final products themselves. Now we hope that you will be inspired not only by the patterns, but also the concepts and stories behind the various motifs.

Christmas is a special time for those of us who live in the north. Winters are dark and cold, and we spend a lot of time sitting by the warm stove with some handwork. For that reason it seemed only natural that our first pattern book should revolve around Christmas and Christmas decorations – we both have a particular weakness for that time of year. Our Christmas workshop has an important place in our home in November and December, when our creativity and joy at making things peak. The concept for this book is quite simple: Christmas balls – one basic pattern with 55 variations. We could have gone on endlessly with this theme, but chose to stop at 55 ornaments. After that, it is up to you to create your own variations in the style you like.

We hope this book will inspire you to have a productive and creative time before Christmas! With our best wishes for a wonderful and happy Christmas,

ARNE & CARLOS

THIS HOMEMADE DOLL HOUSE has a separate room for the Christmas workshop.

CHRISTMAS memories from many parts of the world have found a place in this American trunk.

CHAPTER 1

INTRODUCTION

BY THE END OF OCTOBER the snow sticks on the ground and is here to stay. While this occurs early in the year up here in the mountains, it is not uncommon that we still have a lot of blooms in the meadow. The last colorful flowers covered with a fine layer of snow are such a lovely sight. It happens just as suddenly to us every year, and then we have to rush around the yard and take care of everything that must be done before the really big snow storms come in. Tools and outdoor furniture have to be put in the shed and we have to prepare ourselves for the long winter ahead. It's the time of year when we think about how blessed we are. We are fortunate to live in the country and experience this early snow that covers up all the gray and lights up our everyday lives.

IN THE MIDDLE OF NOVEMBER, we start preparing for the Christmas season. When the first Sunday of Advent arrives we take out the Christmas decorations and plan how to decorate the house. It has to be different from year to year. Old and new purchases and our own handmade Christmas decorations will soon be given their places around the house. We love this time of the year, we take time off to relax, sit back and enjoy the colors, glitter and finery that we have placed throughout the house.

WE COULD EASILY PLAN for Christmas all year. It has to do with expectations – the expectations we had when we were children and sometimes resurface in adults as they get older. When we travel or are just out and about, we always look for more Christmas decorations. It doesn't matter where in the world we find ourselves and what time of year it is. We have come home with angels from Texas, ceramic decorations from Mexico, a wooden Christmas crèche from Peru and numerous glass Christmas balls from Fortnum & Mason as well as Victorian ornaments from the Victoria and Albert Museum in London. We have ransacked flea markets everywhere in the world, always in the hunt for Christmas ornaments – not just objects originally intended as Christmas decorations but other items that can be used for Christmas, such as curtain tassels, fabric remnants, beads on a string, gold fringes, and crystals from old lamps. Yes, there are no limits – anything and everything offers possibilities!

A Christmas Ornament is born

ADVERTISING PHOTO for a Christmas ball designed for Arne&Carlos in collaboration with Comme des Garçons. Now we have a new version of this ball, "Selbu," that you can hand knit.

WE WHO ARE SO BESOTTED WITH CHRISTMAS were honored when, in 2008, we had a commission from Comme des Garçons, Japan's most respected design house. The commission was to design a complete Christmas collection of knitted sweaters, hats, scarves, and neck warmers. Since it was a Christmas collection, we also sent a suggestion with pictures of a little selection of the Christmas balls that we had designed and knit and asked if maybe they wouldn't like to have some. The owner of Comme des Garçons, Rei Kawakubo, liked the Christmas balls so much that she ordered four motifs at once. These were knitted up in Peru on hand knitting machines and sold in her shops in Tokyo, Paris, New York, London, and Hong Kong – and so our little idea about knitted Christmas balls with Nordic motifs became a reality.

And now we've gone one step further and developed the Christmas balls for hand knitting. Of the four original balls, we have only retained ball number 26, "Dancing around the Tree," since it was the only ball that could be knit the same way by hand as by machine. We had to change the pattern for the other three balls so they could be knit by hand. Those were balls 18 "Selbu," 25 "Falling Star," and 50 "Running Reindeer." We then produced 51 completely new designs, so, we now have instructions for a total of 55 balls.

Pattern 17 Selbu

CHAPTER 2

Materials, techniques, and basic instructions

We use Dale of Norway "Heilo" yarn for our knitting. We have tried other yarn types and have found you get a different result from each type of yarn. The biggest difference will be the size of the ornaments, which can vary quite a bit from yarn to yarn. We think the "Heilo" yarn makes a nice size ball if you follow the instructions on page 23. The yarn also makes for easier knitting because the yarn quality is sturdier than many other yarn types we have tried. Since the balls are so small, it is good to knit them in a sturdy yarn. Figure on about .18 oz or five grams of yarn per ball.

If you want to have glittery ornaments, you can use gold or silver novelty yarn. The GGH yarn (Rebecca) "Lame" novelty yarn (62% rayon/38% polyester, 25 g) is thinner than the wool yarn and can make it a little tricky to knit evenly, but, if you are patient, you'll manage just fine.

When the motifs are small, we recommend you embroider them with duplicate stitch instead of knitting them, as on, for example, balls 35 "Harp" or 39 "Anchor" (see section on embroidery, page 29). We used the same yarn for the embroidery as for the knitting.

If it seems too difficult to knit the motifs, you can use the basic pattern to knit some plain ornaments, use a fun novelty yarn instead of the wool yarn. We've knit some balls in different colors of a sparkly Anny Blatt yarn called "Murguet". The yarn is 100% Polyamide that is thin and designed to be knit on needles U.S. size 8 / 5 mm. We used U.S. 2.5 / 3 mm needles with the "Murguet" yarn so the Christmas balls would be the same size as the ones we've knit with wool. If you knit with a different novelty yarn, don't forget it should be a fine yarn in order to use needles U.S. 2.5 / 3 mm. Do a sample before you get going. Many lovely balls can be created this way. You can find out more about the Anny Blatt yarn that we used at www.yarnmarket.com or www.annyblatt.fr .

ALL YOU NEED to make the balls
is yarn, stuffing/batting, knitting
needles, a crochet hook, crystals, a
sewing needle, scale (optional), and
a pair of scissors.

YOU CAN ALSO KNIT CHRISTMAS BALLS with a fun novelty yarn. We were inspired by Christmas fairies and shiny Christmas wrapping paper for these examples and used a sparkly novelty yarn from the French company, Anny Blatt.

IF YOU HAVE BLUE KITCHENWARE, don't despair! The balls can also be knit in colors to match your interior.

Colors

We chose to knit most of our ornaments in white and black or white and red. We have also used gold or silver novelty yarn for some of the balls to have a bit more glitter on the tree. For one ball, we even used a little green, mixed with white and red. Try what you like! Although we think that the white and red or white and black combinations look best on the Christmas tree, there is nothing to stop you from using other colors. We've even knitted some balls in an assortment of colors, with pink, light green, gray, and light blue to show the possibilities are endless. Use your favorite colors and knit the balls in colors that suit you and express your personal style!

We bought a copy of Hans Christian Andersen's *Snow Queen* translated into Lithuanian on a trip to Klaipeda. We knew we had to buy the book when we saw the delightful colors of the illustrations. Those colors inspired the balls shown on this page.

THE FINISHED BALLS weigh about .88 oz/25 grams, and need about .7 oz/20 g wool batting for stuffing.

OUR COLORS AND COLOR NUMBERS:
Dale of Norway "Heilo" (100% wool, 109 yds/ 100 m, 50 g)
Red, 4018
Black, 0090
Off White, 0020
Green, 9145
Blue, 5744

NOVELTY YARN:
GGH (Rebecca) "Lame" (62% rayon/38% polyester, 210 yds, 25 g)
Gold, 100
Silver, 101

Stuffing

WE HAVE EXPERIMENTED with various fillings for our ornaments, such as cotton and acrylic blend batting and pillow stuffing. But, as soon as we discovered 100% wool batts, we found they are perfect for our ornaments because they make them firmer and suppler and they keep their shape. Although this material is more expensive, you need less filling per ball. We used wool batts in natural white but good alternatives are light beige or beige. Avoid a dark colored stuffing as it will show through the balls. Figure on about .70 oz/20 g stuffing per ball.

WOOL CHRISTMAS BALLS can quickly become as glamorous as glass balls if you attach a lot of crystals to them to make them sparkle.

Crystals

ADD A TOUCH OF SPARKLE AND COLOR to your Christmas balls by gluing on some Swarovski crystals. These crystals can actually be ironed on but you risk discoloring or even scorching the wool because it takes a high heat to iron on the crystals. We recommend, you steam the ball, fill it with wool stuffing, and glue on the crystals as the last step. You can find the crystals at your local craft or hobby shops or online at www.firemountaingems.com in mixed colors or clear. We attach the crystals with textile glue and it works quite well. If you are unsure about what type of glue to use, ask the store clerk.

KNITTING NEEDLES AND CROCHET HOOKS

The balls are knit on U.S. size 2.5 / 3 mm needles and the hanging loops crocheted with hook U.S. D-3 / 3 mm. You can work with larger or smaller needles but the balls will be a different size. The size of the needles should be appropriate for the yarn you've chosen. Bamboo needles are the best to use when knitting small items since the stitches won't slide off as easily as with metal needles. You can buy bamboo knitting needles at most yarn stores.

If you knit loosely, try smaller size needles, and, if you knit tightly, try larger needles. The gauge for our balls is 3 sts in 3/8 in / 1 cm. We recommend that you knit a gauge swatch before you begin any of the balls.

COMING SOON - ARNE & CARLOS KITS

In collaboration with Dale of Norway we have designed a beginner's kit with everything you need to get started with the Christmas balls. The kit includes yarn, wool stuffing and a pattern. Check out the Trafalgar Square Books website www.trafalgarbooks.com for updated information where they will be available or at www.arne-carlos.com.

PATTERNS

The motifs we used on the balls, except for those we designed ourselves, can be found in many areas of northern Europe. Norwegian knitting is associated with traditional patterns and "Norwegian motifs," which are readily recognized by the rest of the world.

The eight-petal rose is the pattern most people think of when they hear "Norwegian." This motif is found in every country where people have knitted or woven throughout time. The X's and O's border from the Setesdal sweaters is often considered originally Norwegian but it is also found in German patterns. Reindeer are perhaps the most stereotypical Norwegian motif while the deer is knitted all around Europe. In Peru, the eight-petal rose is knitted along with llamas and pumas.

Knitting expresses both the place and the time you live in. Our patterns come from nature, religion, new trends, tradition and fashion, or they might reflect special origins. Many of the motifs were not originally conceived as Christmas motifs, but we've allowed ourselves the freedom to give them Christmas names, because many of these motifs are associated with Christmas, as, for example, those motifs in the book we call "Decorating the Tree" and "Dancing around the Tree."

Many of the old patterns we've charted, such as "Eight-petal Rose," and "Dovre," have traditionally been knit on mittens. Others, for example, the "Sledding Run" and "Squirrel" are typical motifs from old children's sweaters. Motifs such as "Rocking Horse," "Christmas Pig," and "Squirrel" are ones we designed. They were inspired either by something we have seen, or something we've personally connected with Christmas. No matter what, here's a starting point to take off from and be inspired by!

KNITTING TIPS

None of our motifs have floats of more than 6 stitches between pattern stitches. A float is the strand between two pattern stitches. If there are more than 6 stitches between pattern stitches, twist the yarns on the back of the work. Stagger the places where you twist the yarns so they don't stack over each other—otherwise they will be visible. Stretch the knitting a little so the stranded yarns lay smoothly on the wrong side. This method makes it easier to keep the pattern motifs smooth.

Basic pattern

THIS PATTERN IS THE BASIS for all 55 balls. The charted motif for each individual ball is designed to work within this basic pattern. Don't forget that the charts only show the stitches for ¼ of the ball. The chart stitches are repeated on each of the 4 double-pointed needles. The first row of 3 stitches on the chart represents the 3 cast-on stitches and is not knitted again. The top 3 stitches are not worked either. On the last round, cut the yarn and pull the tail through the remaining 12 stitches, pull tight and weave in tail on WS. Most of the patterns are divided over 4 dpn but some of the balls have patterns only over 2 needles. In that case, the chart shows two repeats side-by-side.

WORK AS FOLLOWS:

RND 1: (the bottom row on the chart with 3 blocks): Cast on 12 sts over dpn US 2.5 / 3 mm. Divide these 12 sts over 4 dpn = 3 sts per ndl.

RND 2: Knit 12.

RND 3: (K2, inc 1, k1) on each ndl. [*Note: see page 27 for how to increase*]

RND 4: Knit 16.

RND 5: (K1, inc 1, k2, inc 1, k1) on each ndl.

RND 6: Knit 24.

RND 7: (K1, inc 1, k4, inc 1, k1) on each ndl.

RND 8: Knit 32.

RND 9: (K1, inc 1, k6, inc 1, k1) on each ndl.

RND 10: Knit 40.

RND 11: (K1, inc 1, k8, inc 1, k1) on each ndl.

RND 12: Knit 48.

RND 13: (K1, inc 1, k10, inc 1, k1) on each ndl.

RND 14: Knit 56.

RND 15: (K1, inc 1, k12, inc 1, k1) on each ndl.

RNDS 16-27: Knit 64.

RND 28: (K1, k2tog, k10, k2tog, k1) on each ndl.

RND 29: Knit 56.

RND 30: (K1, k2tog, k8, k2tog, k1) on each ndl.

RND 31: Knit 48.

RND 32: (K1, k2tog, k6, k2tog, k1) on each ndl.

RND 33: Knit 40.

RND 34: (K1, k2tog, k4, k2tog, k1) on each ndl.

RND 35: Knit 32.

RND 36: (K1, k2tog, k2, k2tog, k1) on each ndl.

RND 37: Knit 24.

RND 38: (K1, k2tog, k2tog, k1) on each ndl.

RND 39: Knit 16.

RND 40: (K1, k2tog, k1) on each ndl.

RND 41 (the top round with 3 blocks on the chart): Do not knit.

Cut yarn, leaving a tail about 8 in / 20 cm long. Pull through the last 12 sts.

ABBREVIATIONS	
BO	bind off (British cast off)
cm	centimeter(s)
CO	cast on
dpn	double-pointed needles
g	gram(s)
in	inch(es)
inc	increase
k	knit
k2tog	knit two together
mm	millimeter(s)
ndl	needle(s)
oz	ounce(s)
rnd	round(s)
RS	right side
st(s)	stitch(es)
WS	wrong side
gauge = British tension	
stockinette = British stocking st	

FINISHING THE BALL: Use the tip of your index finger to push the 12 stitches at the top smoothly together and under at the top of the ball. Thread the yarn once more through all the stitches at the top. Bring the needle and yarn through the hole at the top, secure the yarn by pressing the top towards the hole at the base of the ball and sewing it down securely. Steam the ball and fill with wool batting. Thread the yarn through the stitches at the base, tighten, and tie off yarn. When you fill the ball with wool batting, loosen the wool first so the filling is lofty, and then spread it out well inside the ball. Use the index finger to press in fine layers of wool batting. Don't wad the batting when you are stuffing it in the ball because it will clump up.

Hanging loops

Chain 40, leaving a tail long enough to pass through the whole ball. Finish the chain by joining to the first st with a slip stitch. Pull both tails through the last stitch on the hook and sew the tails through the ball.

KNITTING AND CROCHET BASICS

These step-by-step drawings illustrate the basics for knitting, crocheting the hanging loops, and embroidery techniques that we use:

A. CASTING-ON STITCHES

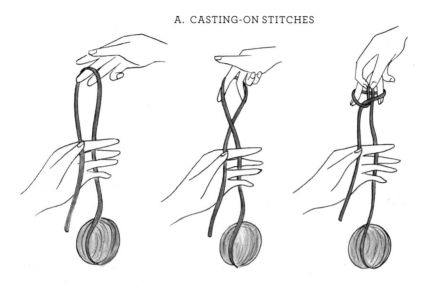

B. MAKE A LOOP OVER THE NEEDLE

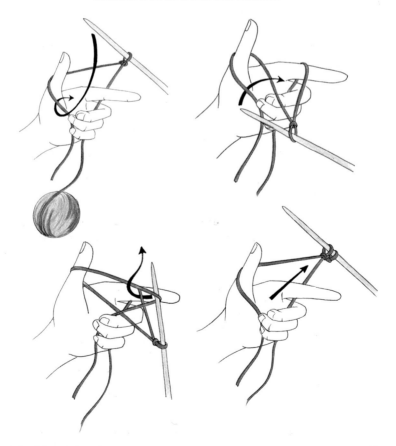

CAST ON 12 STITCHES ONTO ONE NEEDLE AND THEN DIVIDE THE STITCHES OVER 4 DPN.

C. INCREASING

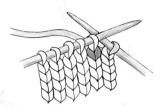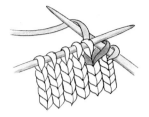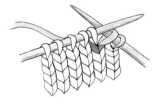

Increase at the beginning of a row by picking up a stitch on the right side of the 2nd stitch on the needle.

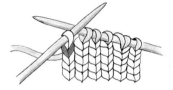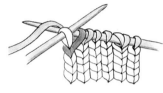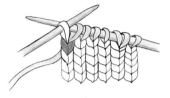

Increase at the end of a row by picking up a stitch in the right side of the last stitch on the needle. This method prevents a hole in the knitting and keeps the stuffing from showing through. Weave in the yarn tails as you work, except for the cast-on tail which you'll need for sewing the hole after the ball is filled with wool batting.

D. DECREASING WHEN ONE STITCH IS A PATTERN STITCH

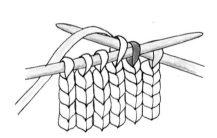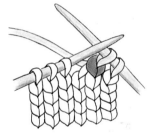

When stitches are to be knit together and the first one of the two is a pattern stitch, insert the needle through back loops, first through stitch 1 and then stitch 2, so that the pattern stitch will lie on top of the decrease.

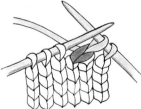

If the pattern stitch is stitch 2 of those to be knit together, knit them together as usual; the needle goes first through stitch 2 and then stitch 1. Pull the working yarn through both stitches.

CROCHETING THE HANGING LOOPS

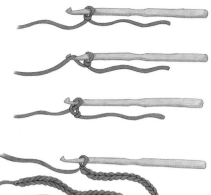

1. **BEGIN BY** making a slip knot loop and placing it on the hook. Tighten slightly but not too much. Make sure the yarn tail is long enough to sew through the ball and fasten. Bring working yarn over the hook and bring it through the loop on the hook. Now you've completed a chain stitch (ch st).

2. **CONTINUE** making chain stitches until you have made 40 sts.

3. **INSERT** the hook in the first chain of the cord.

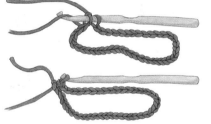

4. **YARN AROUND HOOK** and through both loops on the hook.

5. **CUT WORKING YARN** and bring both yarn tails through the stitch on the hook. Tighten a bit. Now the loop is ready to sew to the ball. Sew both tails through the ball, from top to bottom. Sew the yarns through the ball on each side of the holes at top and bottom. Pull yarn well through the ball, so that the loop sits nicely at the top – not too hard, or you'll have an apple instead of a Christmas ball. Tie the two tails together and sew the ends through the ball. Trim tails and the ball is finished.

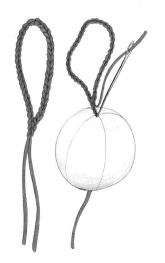

WE LET THE MAIN COLOR of the ball determine the color of the hanging loop. A red background gets a red loop and a white main color has a white loop. This way, the yarns are invisible when the tails are fastened off.

Embroidery instead of pattern knitting

HERE ARE A COUPLE OF BALLS where we've mixed knitting and embroidery.

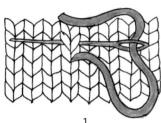

1.

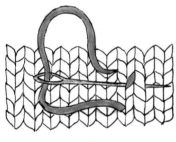

2.

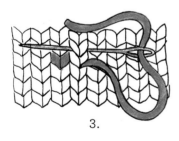

3.

IF YOU FIND KNITTING the motif pattern hard when it's a small or single stitch area and the floats are too long, follow the basic instructions and knit a single-color ball. Use a piece of the yarn to mark where the pattern begins in the center of the pattern repeat on each needle and embroider the motif with duplicate stitches on the ball once you've knitted it.

TIP: Use silk ribbon and tie several balls together and place them around the house. You can also mix pattern knitting with embroidery as we have done on the ball with the heart and crown and the ball with the Christmas bells.

STEAMING THE BALLS

To get the best results for the balls to look nice, we recommend you steam them before you add the stuffing. If you are worried about scorching the balls, place a kitchen towel between the steam iron and the ball.

GLUING ON THE CRYSTALS

Attach the crystals with glue after you have steamed and stuffed the balls. This method is a lot easier than trying to iron them on.

WE PREFER GLUING on the crystals after we've filled the balls with wool. Did you notice Rudolph's shiny red crystal nose in the picture?

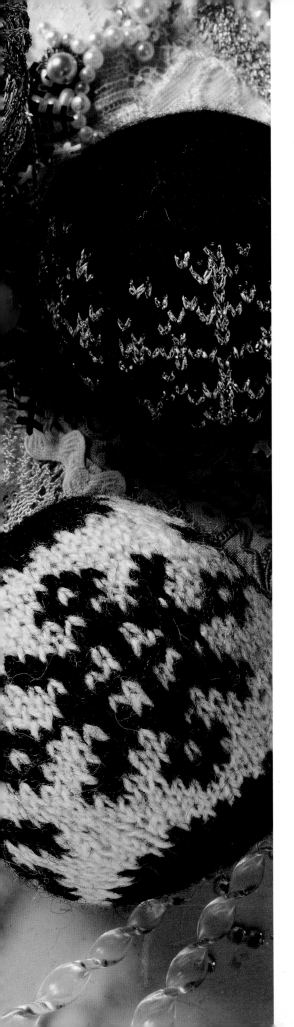

CHAPTER 3

It will be Christmas soon

WHEN THE FIRST SNOW arrives it frees us from all the work in the gardens and fields we've been doing since early spring. The weeds and everything we didn't manage to clean up disappear. The white "frost flowers" cover the ground with sparkly glitter as Christmas nears.

"SNOW CRYSTAL"

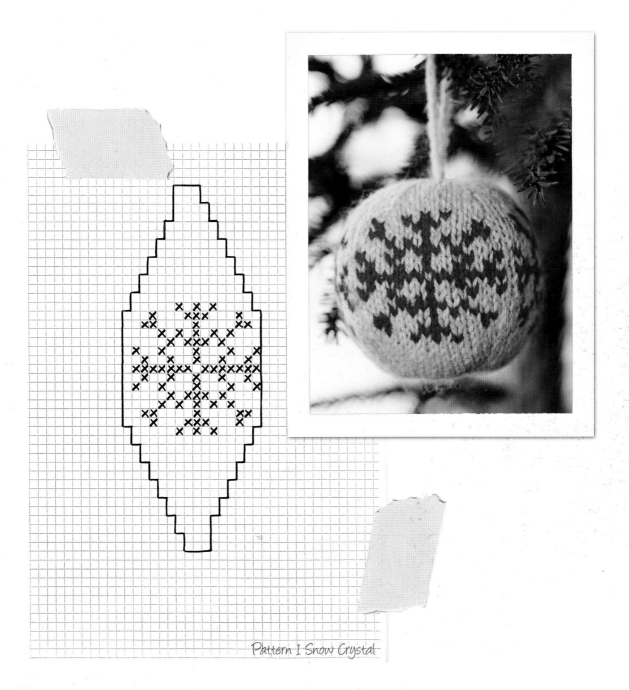

Pattern 1 Snow Crystal

King Winter sprinkles "frost flowers" on the trees, and old houses with wood-sashed windows receive several bouquets in every square. We designed this motif inspired by the frost that sticks to the windows of our studio every winter.

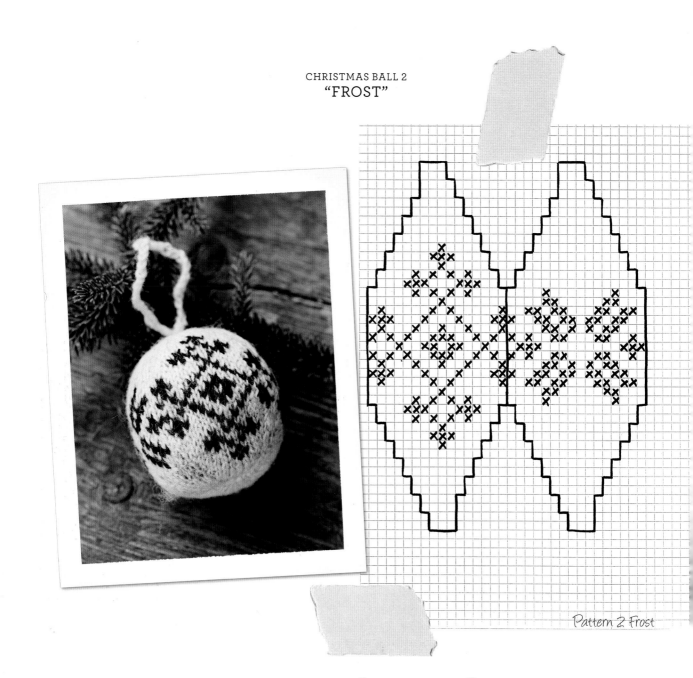

Pattern 2 Frost

Snow crystals or "frost flowers" come in many shapes and maybe some look just like this.

"SNOWFLAKES"

This pattern is very much like the light snow that gently covers a fine and lustrous carpet over the last flowers in the garden which still haven't withered away.

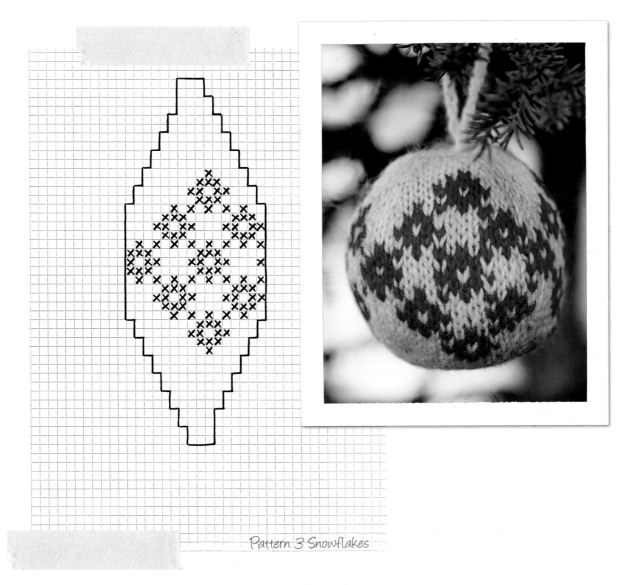

Pattern 3 Snowflakes

Oh, see how it's snowing, oh, see how it's snowing
It will be so much fun, hooray!
Now it's winter, now it's winter
Just like we wanted, hooray!
We'll take the sleds out and put our mittens on
Then we'll climb the hill, hey, away we go!

"OH, SEE HOW IT'S SNOWING" BY FELIX KÖRLING

Pattern 4 New Snow

This snowflake reminds us of the big snowflakes that quietly drift down. We used to call them old troll ladies with spikes in their nose.

CHRISTMAS BALL 5
"SNOWMAN"

The first snowfall always made me happy when I was a little boy. We designed this snowman pattern as a rather simple and childish motif. It represents the wonderful time children have every winter when the first snow falls.

Pattern 5 Snowman

Vi lengter mot hvite vidder og gnistrende
taggete jøkler og blånende åser — eller m...
snetunge graner, kafferast og soldupp i tø...
drypp fra lange istapper.

Vi lengter mot vinterferie!

Og så er ikke spørsmålet om hva vi ska...
sekk langt borte. Det beror selvfølgelig på or...
hytte. Vi tok en runde for å se hva forretni...
og her presenterer vi litt av det store utvalget...

Om ikke annet, så trenge... ...nskje skidrak...
nyelse.

CHAPTER 4

Children's
mittens

SCRAPBOOKS full of inspiration and chests full of old knitting. Everything we have collected proves useful in our studio. Patterns from children's mittens work very well for Christmas balls because the motifs are small.

CHRISTMAS BALL 6
"EIGHT-PETAL ROSE"

We've found the eight-petal rose on many Christmas textiles, printed, woven, and embroidered. Many people have said they associate the eight-petal rose with Christmas. This rose is from a pattern on a child's mitten from the Norwegian Handcraft Association Handcraft shop. We found the booklet with the pattern at the Handcraft shop (Husfliden) in Kristiansand, Norway.

Pattern 6 Eight-Petal Rose

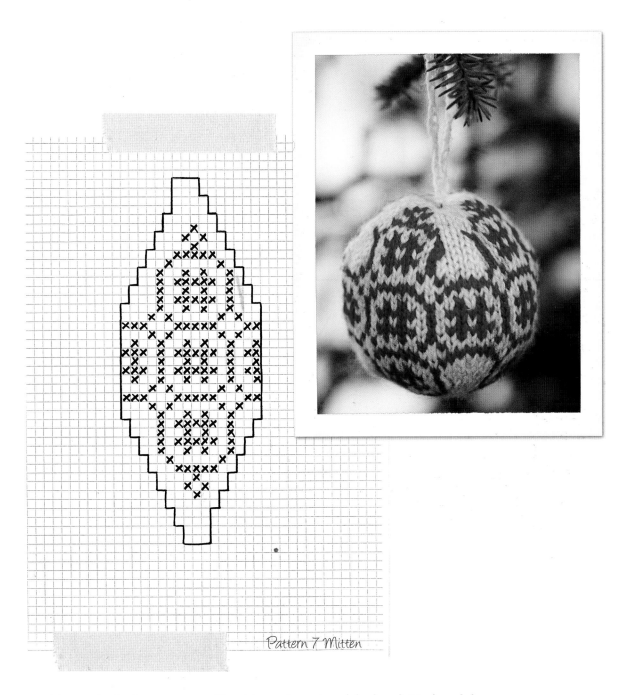

Pattern 7 Mitten

Many mittens have patterns like this on the palm of the hand. We found these crosses on a children's mitten (Norwegian Handcraft pattern 45).

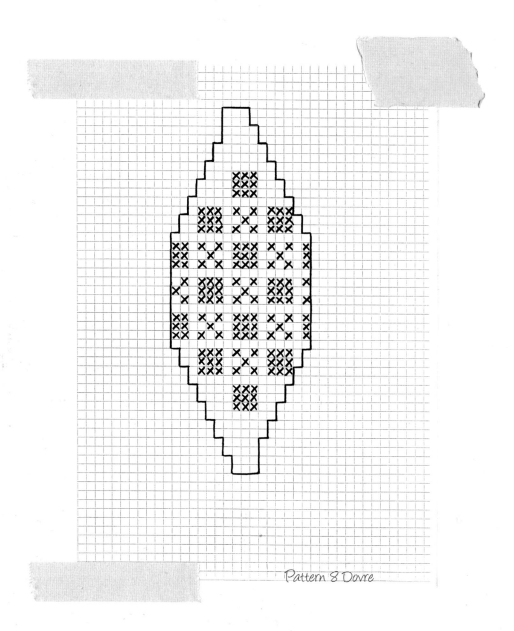

Pattern 8 Dovre

We've seen this pattern in lots of places: a child's mitten from Hallingdal, in German patterns, and on several Latvian mittens. We named it the Dovre ball because Arne's grandfather had a knit jacket with this pattern. We used it on several sweaters and scarves over the years we've worked as knitwear designers. On a Christmas ball, it resembles a pattern on an old glass ornament.

CHAPTER 5

Out on your skis, life's sure to please

HERE'S A COLLAGE for anyone who celebrates Christmas at the ski hut. For those who continue to wear the old sweaters they inherited and use the bamboo poles hanging in the shed. For anyone struggling with back-sliding skis and regretting that they aren't at home knitting on a day like this.

AND THE FOX RACES OVER THE ICE
AND THE FOX RACES OVER THE ICE
NOW CAN WE PLEASE? NOW CAN WE PLEASE?
SING THE LADIES' SONG?

Old folk song

Pattern 9 Tricolor

This motif was inspired by Eskimo sweaters. The pattern, Rauma number 906, was designed for a hat and mittens knitted with Vamse yarn. It is the only Christmas ball we've designed with three colors but that means you can knit many different variations of it. It takes a bit more time to knit this ball because you'll have 3 strands of the colors to manage and they'll want to tangle around each other.

CHRISTMAS BALL 10
"SKI JUMPER"

"We, descendents of the first Norwegians, put on our oil-tanned leather boots, hooded anoraks, "heavy" sweaters, and backpacks, pack the ski wax and four bottles of Golden Cock gin, then sit on the train for four hours until we get to Tonsåsen where winter lasts until spring eases in and takes hold between the spruce trees."

Odd Børretzen: The Norwegian People's Sad Life and History

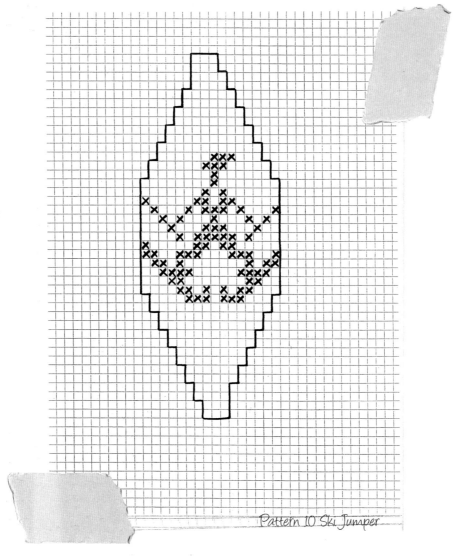

Pattern 10 Ski Jumper

Those of us who live in Tonsåsen take advantage of the fair weather days at Christmas to ski on the old train tracks. We really don't notice the early winter darkness because, the landscape is bathed in a mystical "blue light" that lights our way. We've seen the ski jumper on a vintage ladies' cardigan from the Norwegian handcraft shop and we've also found examples of a similar pattern in traditional Austrian knitting. We used the pattern from the woman's jacket as a starting point but changed it a little so it would fit on the Christmas ball.

CHAPTER 6

Tradition

THE WINTER was cold and the piles of snow got higher. Our ears, fingers, and toes nearly froze. It felt so good to come to the warmth inside, open the oven door of the wood stove, throw in a log and warm our arms and legs. Then we started to feel the frostbite on the tips of our fingers …

WE'VE ALWAYS BEEN inspired by our handcraft traditions which influenced our work when we designed collections for the fashion industry. In the fashion world, everyone is forever caught up with "the latest". For us, to create the "latest" means we have to go back in time, to study our own culture, history, and traditions, select from these elements and use them in a modern way. So not only are we creating the "latest" but also extending our cultural heritage to new generations.

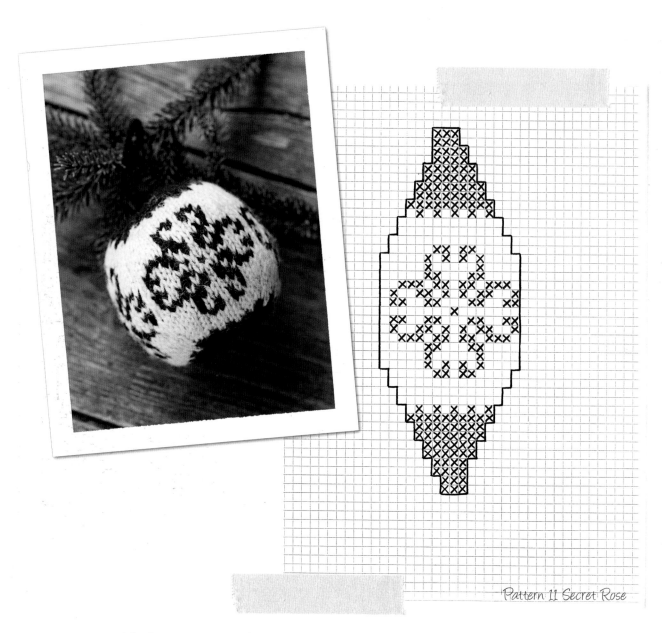

Pattern 11 Secret Rose

A simplified rose pattern is often used, some call it a "secret rose", others the rose of the heart or Selbu Star. Beloved children have many names! This one is from a child's mitten pattern published by the Vestland Handcraft Association.

"HANDCRAFT BORDER"

We found this border pattern in a booklet with a collection of old patterns from the Norwegian Handcraft Association. It is somewhat reminiscent of the patterns found on Eskimo sweaters.

Pattern 12 Handcraft Border

CHAPTER 7

A ski sweater

WE LOVE CLOTHES from the 50's! It was a fantastically creative time in fashion history when all sorts of garment styles were explored.

We find very little that is original in today's styles. Whenever we do notice something that looks new and exciting in the fashion pages, we can always trace its antecedents to old books from the 50's.

When it comes to ski sweaters, we have a special weakness for the 50's styles with geometric, Norwegian-inspired motifs. The pictures in our inspiration book come from an old handcraft magazine. The knitted swatch is the last remnant of an old and worn-out jacket.

"CHRISTMAS STOCKING"

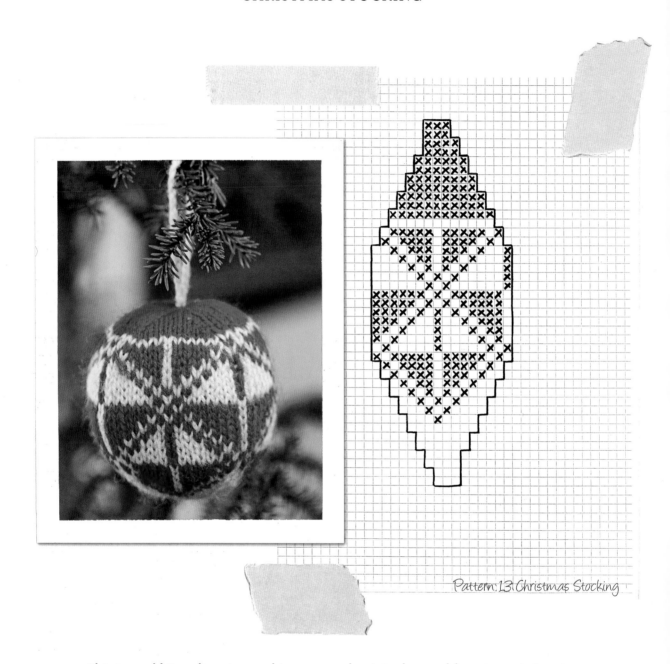

Pattern 13 Christmas Stocking

This is an old Scandinavian stocking pattern, but it is also used for mittens in Latvia. Other than that, we have no idea where the pattern came from. What we do know is that it works perfectly on a Christmas ball!

Pattern 14 X's and O's version 1

Many people are immediately reminded of Setesdal sweaters when they see this X's and O's pattern, as it is called. The cross is an Andrew's cross and the circles are the wheel of life or the sun.

"X'S AND O'S VERSION 2"

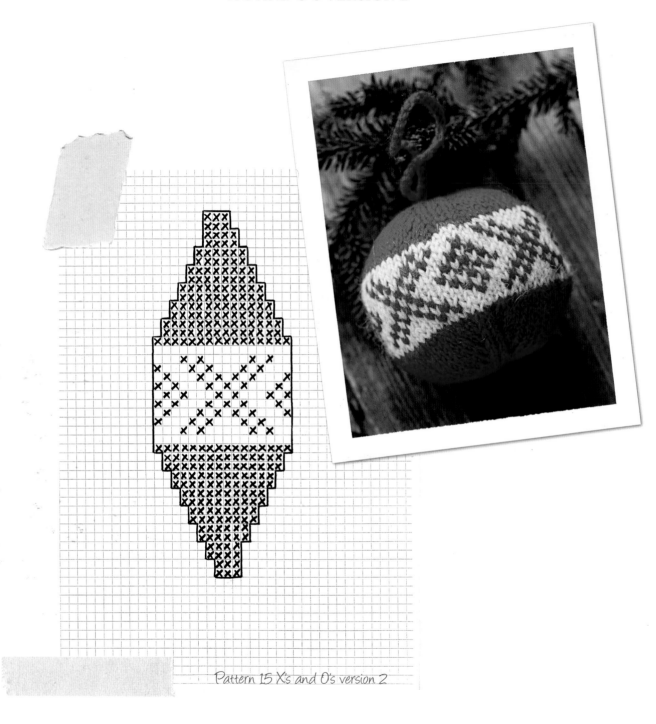

Pattern 15 X's and O's version 2

Here's another version of one of Norway's most recognized and used motifs. It is easier to knit than version 1 because it doesn't have "lice" at the top and bottom.

"HALLING BORDER"

In Annichen Sibbern Bøhn's book, *Norwegian Knitting Designs* (1947), this pattern is called "Halling border." We used half of the border for our ball. We've also used the same pattern in our previous work. Among other things, we designed a sweater with batwing sleeves for our series of hand knitted designs exclusively for Norsk Flid in 2007.

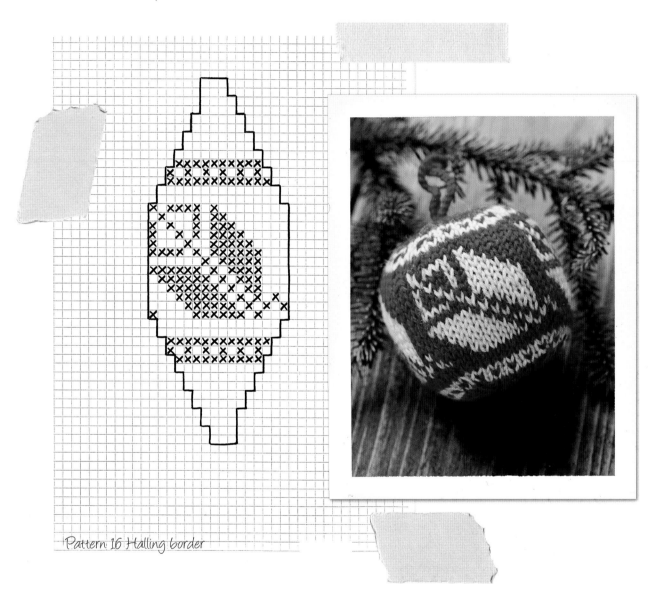

Pattern 16 Halling border

CHAPTER 8

Christmas greenery

WE COLLECT antique metal Christmas tree stands. With so many stands in our collection, we don't have to go looking for one every Christmas. This large stand made of cast iron with holly and berries is one of the loveliest we own. That tree stand has inspired several Christmas flower motifs on the ornaments.

This pattern is frequently featured on Selbu mittens so, of course, we've named the ball Selbu. The Selbu motif reminded us a little of holly but it is actually a four-leaf clover. We've seen the same pattern on a woman's sweater in the 1948 knitting book *Women and Clothing*.

Pattern 17 Selbu

"THREE LEAF CLOVER"

Pattern 18 Three-Leaf Clover

This motif has popped up in several places, on the thumb of a Selbu mitten and on a Latvian border. When knitting this ball, you'll have to twist the strands around each other so the floats won't be too long. Otherwise, the long floats quickly start to pull in the knitting.

"POINSETTIA"

The largest poinsettia that Arne had ever seen was behind the greenhouse at the agricultural college in Klones where it has always been a goal to keep the poinsettias alive in the garden until spring. As we all know, it isn't the easiest thing in the world to keep a poinsettia alive. It can't tolerate too much water or too little, and it often looks like it will give up the second Christmas is over. However, if you manage to keep it alive, you'll be rewarded with a little bush.

Carlos had never seen such little poinsettias as those we buy for Christmas here in Norway but then he grew up under a poinsettia hedge in Brazil.

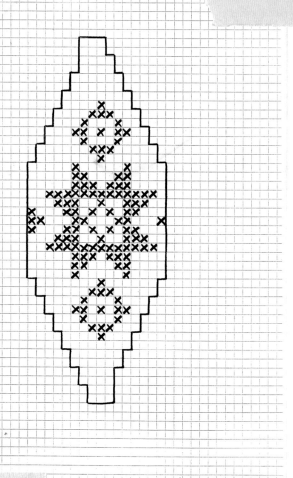

Pattern 19 Poinsettia

If you are going to give a rocking horse as a present, it can be difficult to wrap it nicely. We've decorated this lovely old rocking horse with spruce branches and tied a Christmas ball around its neck. It looks perfect in front of the Christmas tree!

Gott Nytt År

Gott Nytt År
tillönskas av

CHAPTER 9

December 23: Little Christmas Eve

DECEMBER 23 is the day to clean the house, pack the cookies into tins, and make sure you have all the Christmas packages ready. It's also time to get the tree and prepare it for trimming. There's a lot to do on this day and evening but, if you are lucky, maybe you'll have enough time to knit a couple of Christmas balls before the evening is over.

"SLEDDING RUN"

Pattern 20 Sledding Run

Some people are lucky and can find their Christmas tree in the forest on Little Christmas Eve and bring it back home on a sled. And if your tree isn't too big there might be room left on the sled for you.

We found the toboggan motif on a children's sweater from the Norwegian Handcraft Association, pattern 147. This ornament will sparkle if you glue clear crystals in the falling snow or embroider the flakes with silver thread.

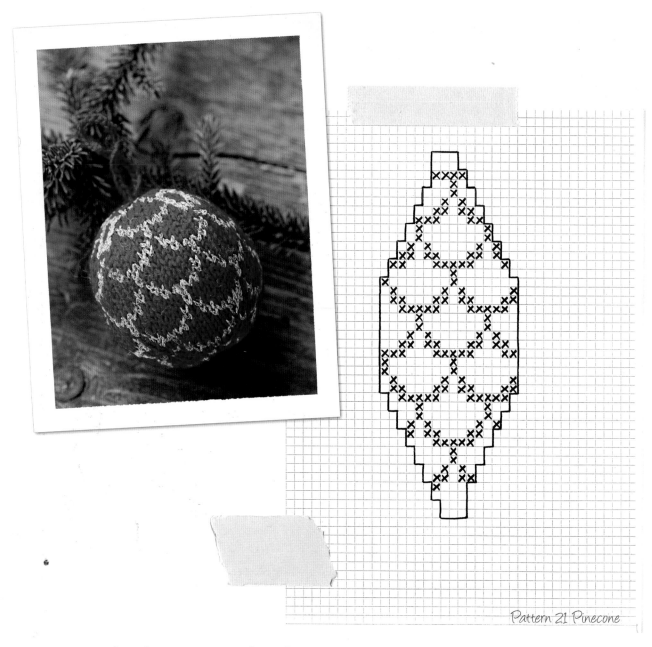

Pattern 21 Pinecone

We drew this pinecone motif ourselves. It was inspired by an old glass pinecone-shaped Christmas tree ornament that we have at home. This ball will be lovely no matter what colors you choose for it. We have knitted versions in red and gold, white and silver, and black and white. It's an easy and fun ball to knit!

"CHRISTMAS TREE"

This Christmas tree ball is our own design. You can also knit it in green and white, embroidering the branches with gold and silver or you can glue on some crystals. There are long floats at the top of the pattern so remember to twist the strands as you knit and never strand with more than 6 stitches in between.

Pattern 22 Christmas Tree

"DECORATING THE TREE"

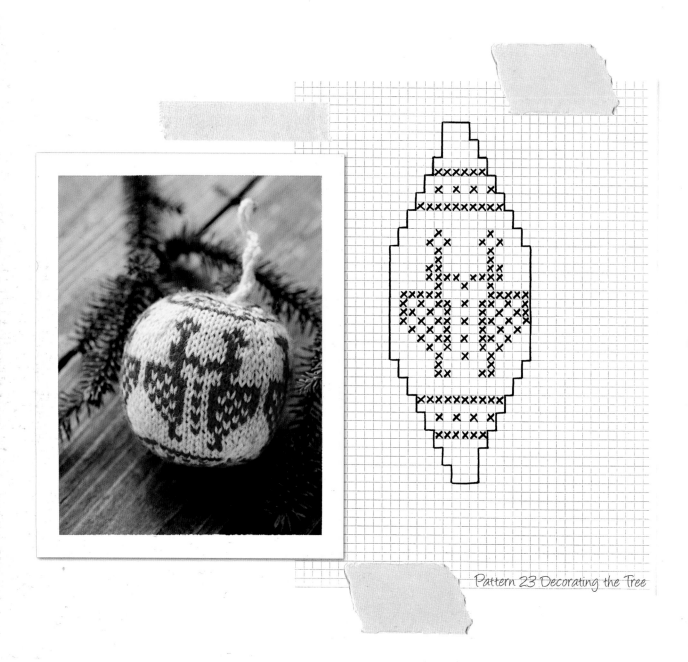

Pattern 23 Decorating the Tree

We always decorate our tree late in the evening of December 23 so, on Christmas Eve we wake up to a completely decorated house. We found the motif for this ball on an old mitten from the Handcraft Association. It wasn't originally a Christmas design but the ladies appear to be decorating a tree with tinsel or garland. In any case, we thought it was quite appropriate for Christmas.

It doesn't matter what the
tree looks like, every tree is
beautiful with decorations.

CHAPTER 10

The night before Christmas

Give your knitting a rest on this day if you can. As we know from the traditional Swedish Christmas song, Christmas lasts until Easter – that means you have time for knitting from Christmas day through spring. These antique Russian dolls are celebrating Christmas under the tree and remind us of the "dancing girls" border on the Christmas ball we call "Dancing around the Tree."

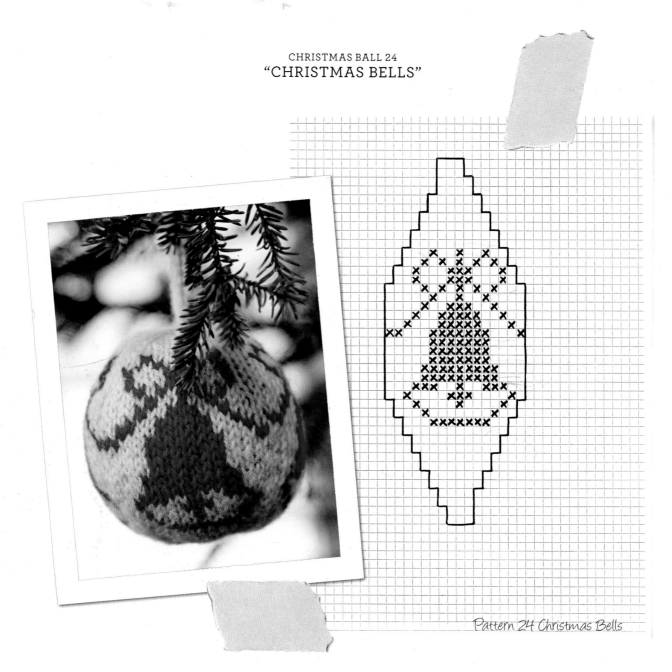

Pattern 24 Christmas Bells

We always heard the church bells when they rang in Christmas at 5 o'clock. It was dark and a little gloomy outside. If there was anything we were sure about at 5 in the morning was the Christmas elf wasn't far away. Maybe he was standing in the barn door and listening to the bells as we were, as we stood at the threshold of our house?

Soon we will hear
The bells proclaiming
And announcing the feast time in our homes.
Soon we'll hear the ringing,
And they will chime in
Christmas for everyone – in heart and mind.

"On to Christmas" by Margrethe Munthe

USE YOUR HAND KNITTED
Christmas balls to deco-
rate the outside of a present. Attach the ball with
silk ribbon for a personal
touch on the gift and then
you'll be giving two presents in one.

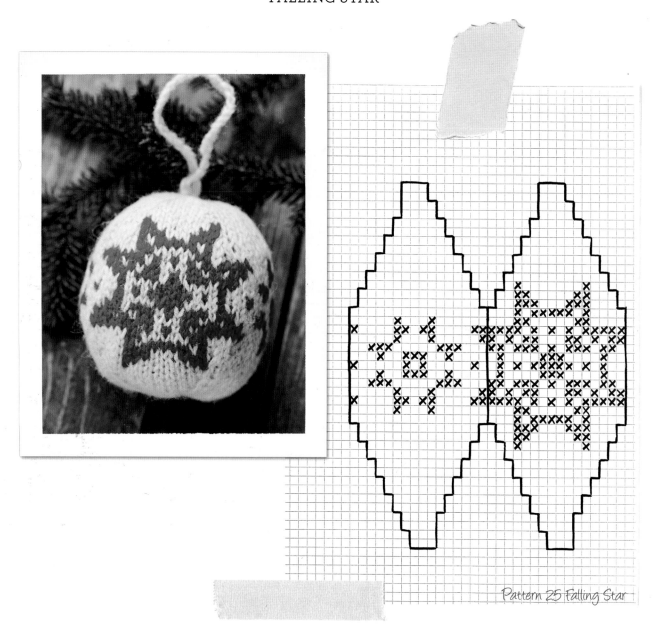

Pattern 25 Falling Star

The motif on this Christmas ball is usually called the "eight-petal rose" but, because it has pointed rather than rounded edges, we think it looks more like a "falling star".

Pull the bench up to the window, and we're all set to gaze,
to search and discover where the Christmas star is,
the shiniest star of all, she is so clear and large
—you need to look over the horizon where the Earth mother Matja lives.

"Christmas Eve poem" by Alf Prøysen

"DANCING AROUND THE TREE"

This motif reminded us of dancing around the tree, that's how the name came about. And it's also this very Christmas ball that started the whole project. As you can imagine it's very special to us.

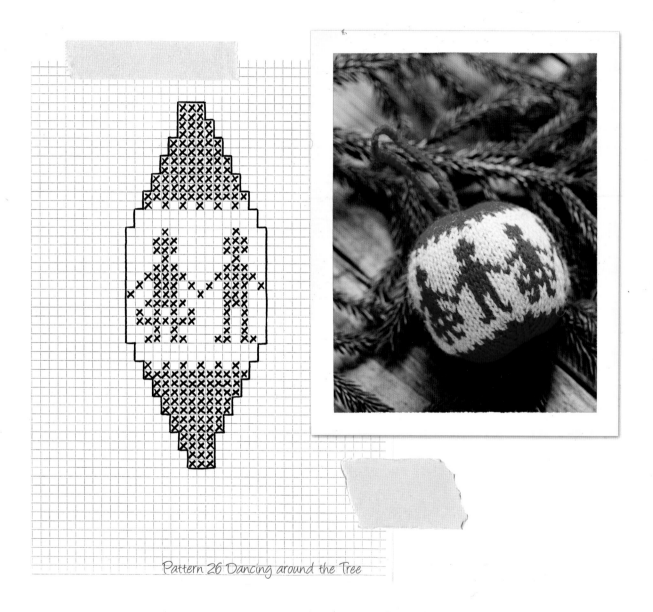

Pattern 26 Dancing around the Tree

At the Christmas tree festival, the tree looks huge for anyone who is little. When the tree is lit the people hold hands and dance to the right and to the left on every other turn, rocking both the tree and the floor. At home we might have had a "wall" tree, which could have been a tree with branches on just one side. This type of tree stood in the corner or against a wall and didn't sway, in fact it was often attached to the ceiling so it wouldn't. Everyone held hands and swayed side to side and sang, "Greetings, green and glittering tree."

CHRISTMAS IS the most fun for little children. Here's how we decorated the children's room in our homemade doll's house.

"ROCKING HORSE"

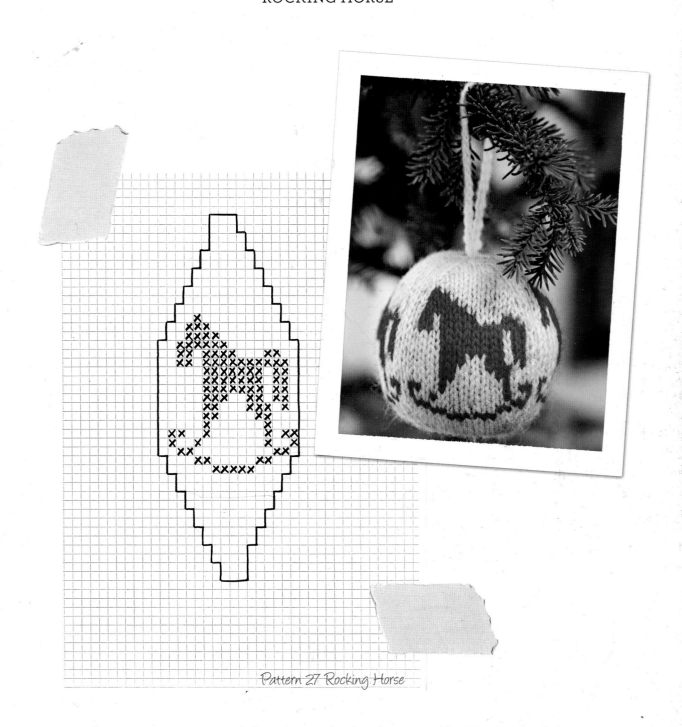

Pattern 27 Rocking Horse

When we were younger, we left our list out for the Christmas elf. We're not sure if the elf got our list each Christmas, they may have blown away in the wind. Rocking horses have appeared under many a tree for generations as gifts, if you have an heirloom rocking horse place it beside the tree and decorate it with ribbons, greenery and ornaments. The rocking horse symbolizes good luck and prosperity!

CHAPTER 11

Christmas goodies

"In the old days, you would be satisfied with a simple treat for Christmas, but in the 1970's, we discovered Saturday sweets/candy, and it has been a long time now since an orange was enough to save Christmas. The box of peppermint pigs is almost empty and Christmas isn't over yet."

Pattern 28 Peppermint Pigs

This ball was inspired by the old glass ornaments that came in every imaginable color combination. We knitted the first one in red and white and it looked a peppermint candy that Scandinavians call a "peppermint pig" – a sugar textile on the tree! These balls can be knitted in any color you like or that suits your style. Make sure you don't pucker the ball too much as you knit. Since the pattern goes all the way around, it is easy to pull in too much when you knit and then the hole at the bottom will be too small, making it difficult to fill the ball with the wool stuffing.

CHRISTMAS TREATS
are not just candy – at
Christmas we make all
sorts of traditional foods.
Tip: Decorate the table
festively: set the table
with your finest linens
and your best silverware.
Place a Christmas ball on
each napkin so the guest
can take one home, it
makes a lovely memento
from Christmas dinner.

CHRISTMAS BALL 29
"CHRISTMAS PACKAGE"

These heart shapes remind us of the small colorful baskets filled with candies that people used to hang on Christmas trees in the old days.

Pattern 29 Christmas Package

GRANDMOTHER'S CHRISTMAS

"I remember the time before Christmas when I went to the store to buy paraffin for the lamps. There were a lot of young people at the store and everyone was buying sweet apples and oranges. I really wanted some oranges, too. So, with fruit on my mind, I put the paraffin can on the counter and asked for oranges! The storekeeper smiled and asked from behind the counter, "How can I get them into that can there?" I remember how embarrassing it was. I was quick to say that it was paraffin I needed. When grandmother came home from Follebu, she had presents for all of us little ones. There were oranges, apples and sugar treats. On Christmas night we ate all the treats grandmother had brought. We also received clothing. It was usual to receive so many gifts, because times were hard for people then. Father read the Christmas story every Christmas and we had to sit still and listen. There wasn't any radio or TV, so we entertained ourselves. We children danced around the tree and made a terrific commotion."

Magnhild Skatrud – Arne's grandmother

FIND A NICE BOX and fill it with Christmas balls. It will be a personal and thoughtful gift. Our box came from the Sacher patisserie in Vienna and holds 9 balls perfectly.

CHAPTER 12

Hearts

Hearts appear everywhere at Christmas, including knitted hearts and woven ones. Many shuttles are embellished with hearts and perhaps were a lover's gift in the old times. We were inspired by our collection of old weaving shuttles and made four Christmas balls with heart motifs.

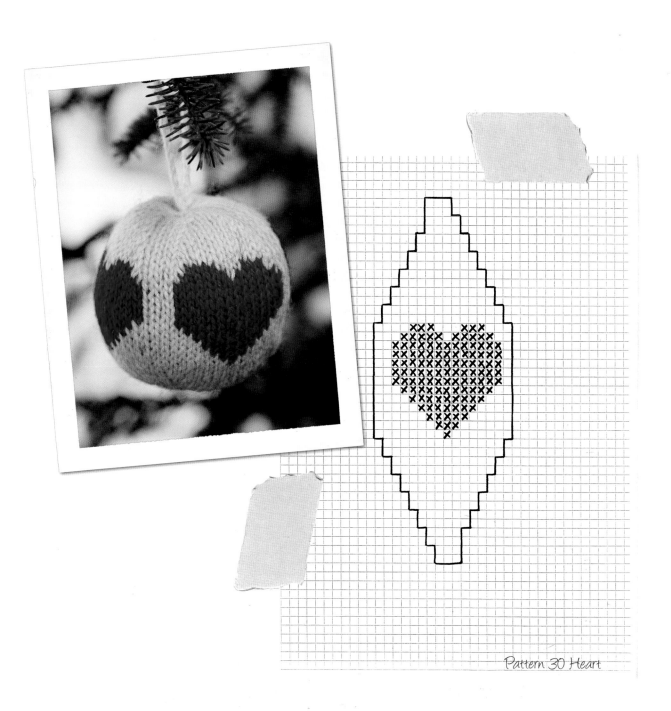

Pattern 30 Heart

A simple heart, embellished with 16 crystals artfully arranged over the knitted heart.

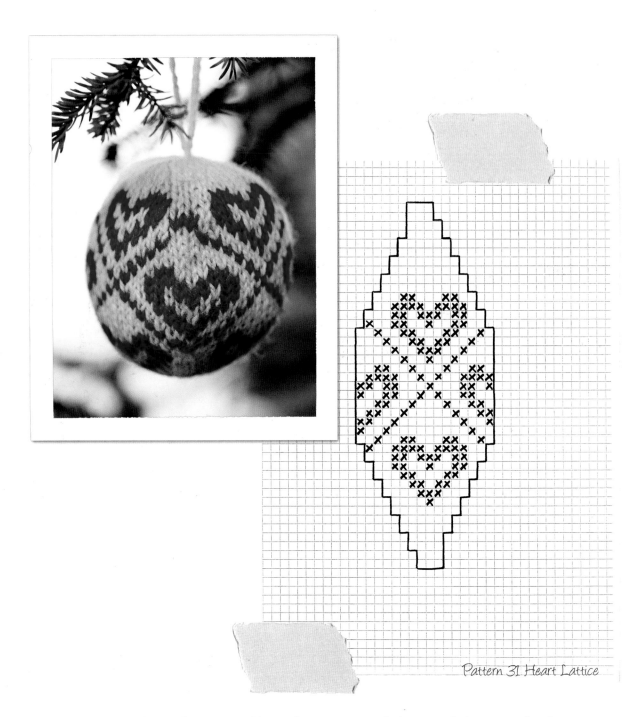

Pattern 31 Heart Lattice

We've found the staggered heart design in several places, including an Icelandic pattern. The hearts look like they are packed in little baskets just like the candy baskets found on an old-fashioned Christmas tree.

"HOSPITALITY: ROOM IN THE HEART"

Pattern 32 Hospitality

Four hearts come together in this pretty ornament. Where there is room in the heart, there is room in the home.

"MEETING HEARTS"

Inspiration can be found in many places: the design on this Christmas ball might remind you of a belt buckle, with two hearts that meet.

Pattern 33 Meeting Hearts

Tip: Make a wreath to put on your front door and decorate it with Christmas balls. The wreath shown here is made with birch branches and shaped into a heart. The balls with the hospitality motif make a lovely welcome to all your Christmas guests. When the balls are filled with 100% wool, they'll hold up outside just fine.

CHAPTER 13

The choir of angels

HE LAY THERE with hay for his pillow
and cried in his humble bed,
but the angels sang outside
on Bethlehem's deserted meadow.

"Christmas Eve" by Jakob Sande

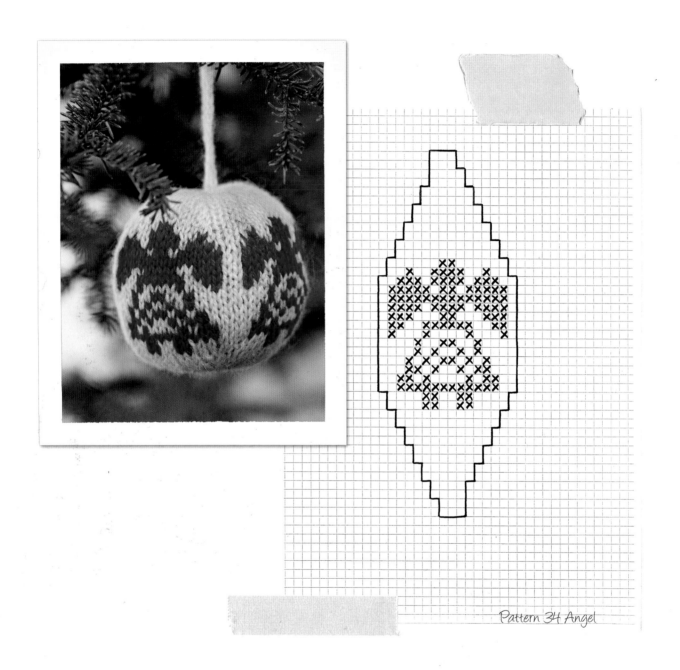

Pattern 34 Angel

We bought an old postcard album at the flea market in Paris and found a card featuring two musical angels. They looked like two very old angels we had that laid in a box year-round because they were too fragile to hang up on the tree. The box was put away and we are still trying to find it. So it goes... the angels on this ball remind us of our poor angels that disappeared.

"HARP"

We designed the motif on this ball in honor of the beautiful miniature instruments we bought at the Victoria and Albert Museum in London. They are copies of old Victorian Christmas ornaments from the museum's collections. We have a harp, a violin, and a mandolin that usually earn the prime spots on the Christmas tree. This collection of Victorian Christmas ornaments is our favorite. The ball with the harp looks easy but the motif is rather small, and means there are some long floats. Don't forget to twist the strands around each other as you knit.

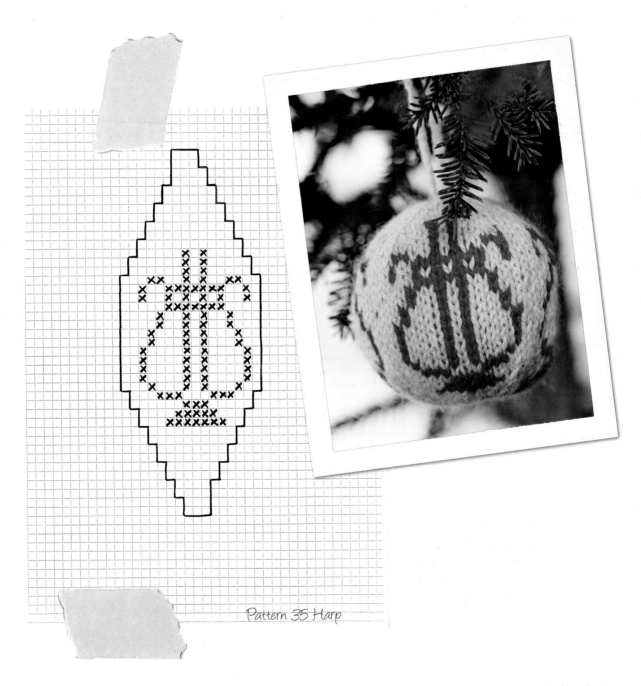

Pattern 35 Harp

CHAPTER 14

Religious motifs

WE CELEBRATE CHRISTMAS in memory of the birth of Jesus, so it's natural to use religious symbols on some of the ornaments. We've selected a few with universal religious meanings.

CROWN

Pattern 36 Crown

We've noticed crowns appear frequently on Christmas ornaments as we visit shops around the world. We found the motif in a Selbu knitted pattern and also in a design from Spain. The crown reminds us of the king who was born and the Virgin Mary who is often depicted wearing a crown. The Christmas ball with the crown can be made especially lovely if embellished with crystals or embroidery.

"LILY"

The lily symbolizes the Holy Trinity and the announcement Mary received from the Archangel. This symbolic motif is often seen in interior design textiles so we thought it would also be appropriate for a Christmas ball.

Pattern 37 Lily

CHRISTMAS BALL 38
"BUTTERFLY"

The butterfly is a religious symbol for rebirth. The motif provides ample room for many variations and you can decorate it with embroidery or glue on crystals. Or, maybe you want to check your stash and create a colorful butterfly—the butterfly world is open to many colors.

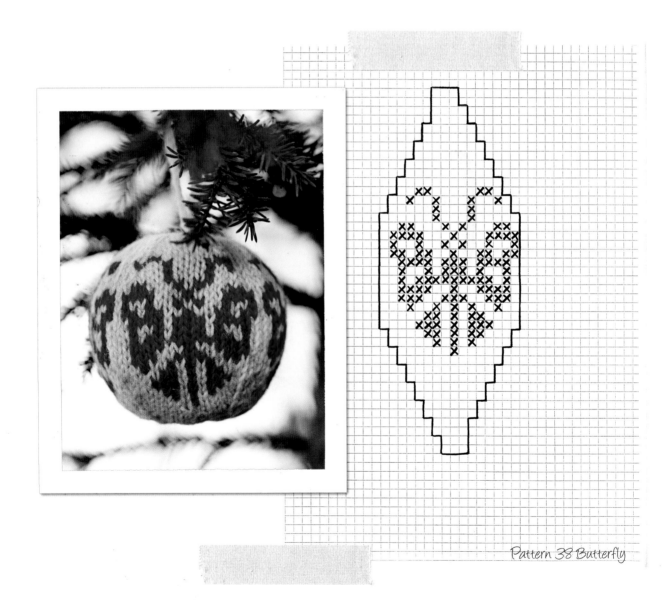

Pattern 38 Butterfly

Pattern 39 Anchor

We found this anchor motif on a woman's sweater in an old knitting book from the Norwegian Weekly Journal, called the Sweater Book. We drew a smaller version that would fit on a Christmas ball. It would be simpler to embroider this motif with duplicate stitch onto a single-color ball. Otherwise, there are many long floats and the knitting can easily pull in.

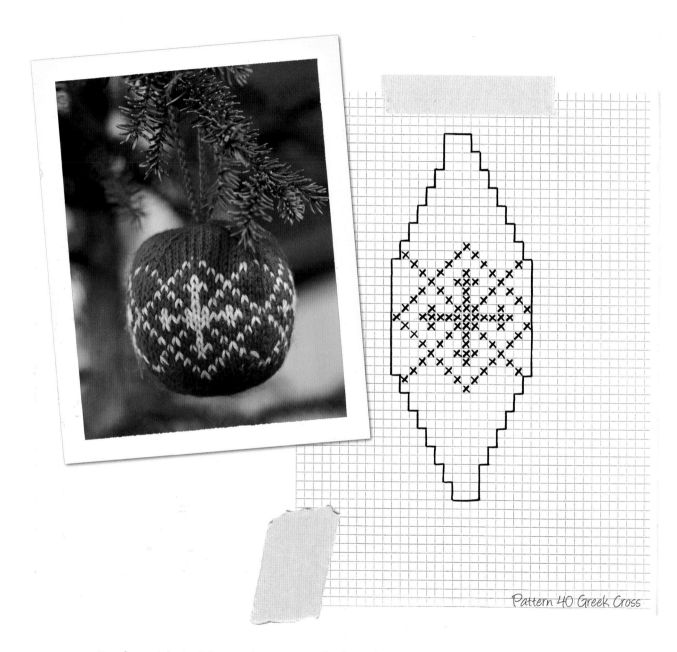

Pattern 40 Greek Cross

One late night in Athens, when we were looking for something to eat in what appeared to be a doubtful spot, we passed a small church with the door slightly open. We got a little glimpse of a world filled with light, colors, and song, a closed world with the door ajar. This is the spirit we want for Christmas. It's the atmosphere we create with the warmth and glow from living light, some religious figures, and old Christmas songs playing on vinyl records. When the smell of Christmas food and incense is added, the atmosphere is perfect. We have chosen to call this ball Greek Cross because it is similar to, and reminiscent of, that moment in Athens.

"CROWN AND HEART"

This motif was drawn following a pattern in the book, *Invisible Threads in Knitting* by Annemor Sundbø. It will be even lovelier if you embellish it with duplicate stitch using gold and silver thread. A silver crown and a heart of gold! Select some of the stitches and embroider over them.

Pattern 41 Crown and Heart

CHAPTER 15

Animals & birds

People used to believe that animals could talk on Christmas night. No one could report that they actually heard them talking, but, just to be sure what the animals said would be nice, it was best to take good care of the animals that evening.

CHRISTMAS BALLS for the animals. The birds get their own for Christmas, we hang little nets filled with food and doughnuts decorated with red silk ribbons.

"BIRD ON A BRANCH"

Pattern 42
Bird on a Branch

Should they be so forgotten
Those who now in snow and sleet
Must always live outside
And survive with so little to eat.

LITTLE BIRDS by Marie Hamsun

Pattern 43 Christmas Pig

The midwinter night is cold. Sparks
from the stars sprinkle all over.
Desolation lies in a farmer's yard.
Everyone inside is sleeping.
The moon makes its circle in back.
The white snow shines on the trees and roofs;
Whiteness covers meadows and fields.
Only an elf is watching.

THE ELF by Viktor Rydberg

THE PIG AND THE MOON

The Christmas pig often had a good start in life. He lived in a basket by the hearth and was fed with his own spoon. He was fattened up until he got too big for the hearthside and had to move out of the house and in together with the other animals. When it got close to Christmas, he was only secure when the moon waned. Everyone knew that he couldn't meet his end when the moon was waning because the meat would shrink in the roasting pan. If the meat shrank, you had only yourself to blame because you fooled with the moon. It was a good idea to have an almanac on hand; a pig's keeper always had to bargain with the moon.

We have made this doll house especially to illustrate the story about the pig.

CHRISTMAS BALL 44
"BULLFINCH"

It is not just people who overeat at Christmas. Many a bullfinch has fallen off the perch outside the kitchen window after eating too much food. Just like a person who can't manage to stop when there is something good to eat. When the bullfinch doesn't have any sense and we see him sitting there too long, we have to shoo him away from the doughnuts and seeds.

Pattern 44 Bullfinch

Pattern 45 The Squirrel

We found this squirrel on a vintage children's outfit and we drew our own design. A visit by the squirrel is part of Christmas here and we hope he stays until spring.

We had a squirrel that used to come to the bird feeder every Christmas for many years. He even hung around well into spring. There were a lot of nuts in the feeder since there aren't that many nut-eating animals here. In the early years he was a spry little rascal that ran around the house along a decorative molding and sat on the waterspout. The last time we saw him, he had gray down his back, and couldn't run the same way along the molding anymore. He didn't come back the next Christmas.

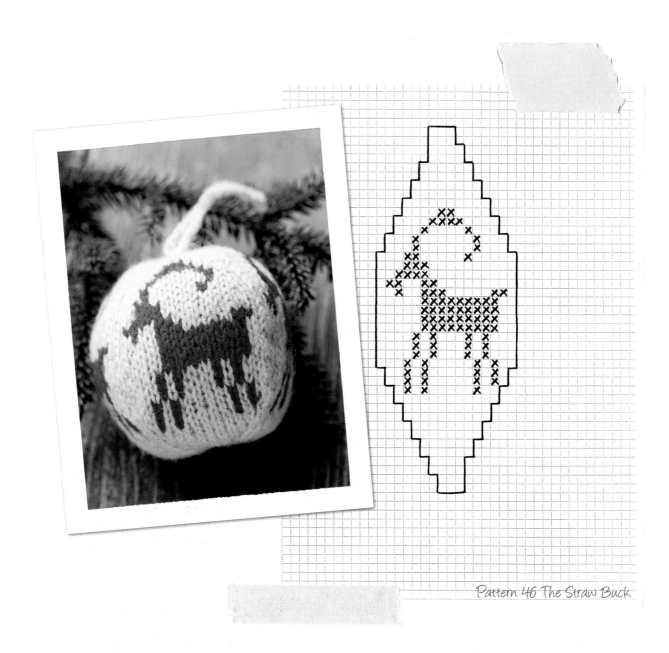

Pattern 46 The Straw Buck

Straw Christmas decorations should remind us of Jesus who was born in a stall. Sweden has the longest tradition of making straw Christmas ornaments. We have an old straw buck.

The Christmas Buck

GOING OUT ON THE CHRISTMAS BUCK ROUNDS in disguise could be quite unpleasant. It certainly wasn't fun to have old stocking legs squeezed down over our heads and pulled in so tightly that our faces lost all circulation. With the blood flow stopped, our faces froze. Being afraid of the dark, we never dared to go further than the nearest neighbor's house because outside lamps lit up most of the way there but not beyond. None of us would even try to pretend to sound like the Christmas buck because they would recognize you immediately and singing Christmas carols was something only young Americans did. At that time we hadn't even heard about American kids; that came later in movies. So we stood there and silently waited until someone or another opened the door and came out on the steps and said something like: "Oh, if it isn't the Christmas bucks, look at how cute they are!" and they went in again and closed the door, as there was no way that anybody would stand out in the cold just to hear us sing "The elf is sitting on the barn". Winter nights were cold at that time of year, always. So we went home in our way-too-big shoes, pulled off our stockings, got our faces thawed out, and the entertainment was over. Teenagers did venture further away, maybe to an aunt's house where they could go into the living room and show their sweetheart what their relatives looked like. But they didn't go around with stockings pulled over their heads; instead, they wore masks bought in Lillehammer – masks of sweet little old troll women with red cheeks or fake noses with moustache and glasses. They looked a bit more professional and maybe they would go on to the Christmas buck party and win the fruit basket for best costume. Maybe their aunt gave them oranges to take with them, or if nothing else, there were always some left over doughnuts to take. So they disappeared out in the dark, giggled and talked about who was who of those they saw inside in the living room or kitchen. Those teenagers were not afraid of the dark. Eventually the Christmas buck tradition disappeared. People no longer dared to let anyone inside in the middle of the night because you never know what or who is coming down the road.

CHAPTER 16

Reindeer

The reindeer is one of our most favorite motifs. This chapter features two of our own reindeer designs and two traditional ones.

"REINDEER HEART"

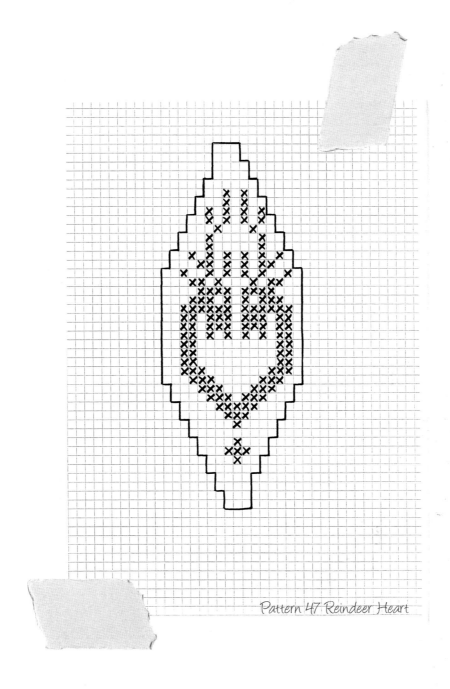

Pattern 47 Reindeer Heart

We designed this reindeer head for our first knitwear collection. Ever since then reindeer have been with us in one form or another. When you place two of these heads side by side, they make a pretty heart.

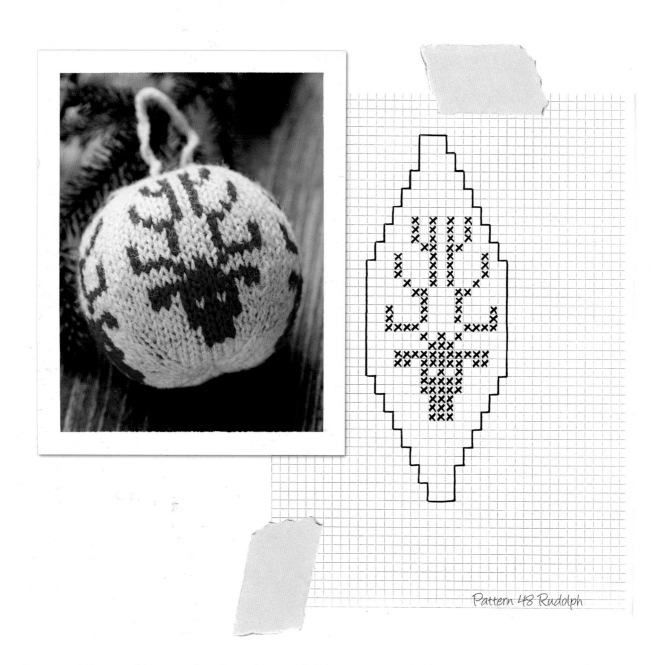

Pattern 48 Rudolph

What would Santa Claus be without Rudolph? You can make this Christmas ball really fun by using a red crystal for the nose. We've also used this design on sweaters in previous collections with the motif worked in knit and purl relief stitches.

CHRISTMAS ORNAMENTS don't have to be reserved only for decorating the tree. We made a Christmas mobile with three reindeer antlers that we joined into a triangle and suspended from the kitchen ceiling and we hang mostly reindeer motif balls on it.

CHRISTMAS BALL 49
"REINDEER"

Pattern 49 Reindeer

A very popular and old reindeer motif; found on sweaters, mittens, and hats. We lengthened the legs a bit so the reindeer will look nicer on the Christmas ball.

CHRISTMAS BALL 50
"RUNNING REINDEER"

This reindeer has run across many a mitten.
We have four in our herd here.

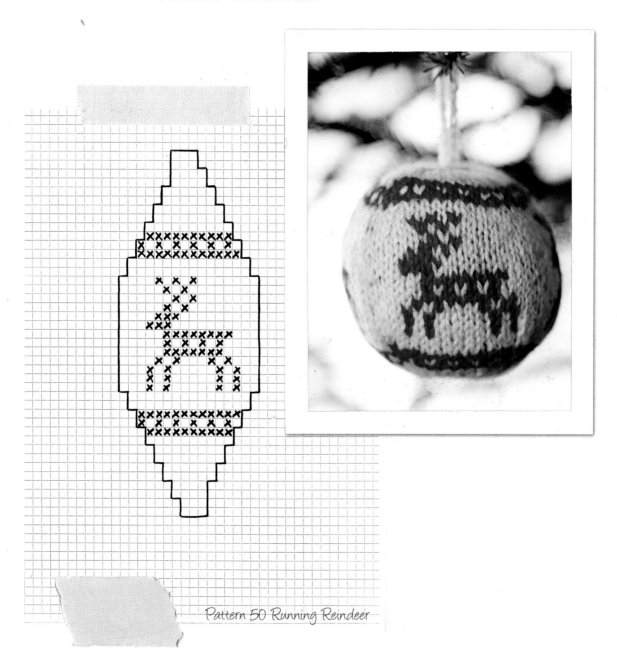

Pattern 50 Running Reindeer

CHAPTER 17

Light

WHEN A THOUSAND CHRISTMAS
LIGHTS ARE LIT
They shine around our world
As the heavenly stars shine down
on everything large and small.

WHEN A THOUSAND CHRISTMAS
LIGHTS ARE LIT
by Emmy Köhler

"ANGEL WITH CANDLE"

We've seen angels like this in old Scandinavian patterns. However, we don't know where our angel came from originally, since we drew her a long time ago. In any case, it is an angel with a candle, a very suitable motif for a Christmas ornament.

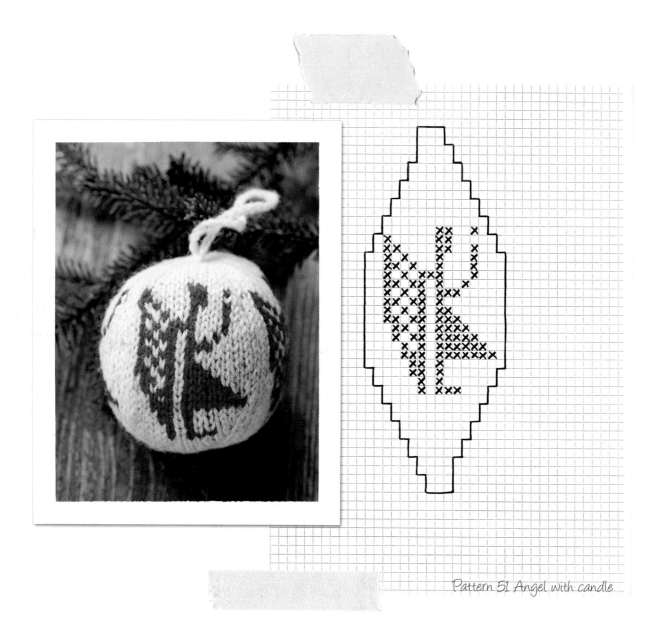

Pattern 51 Angel with candle

"CHRISTMAS LIGHT"

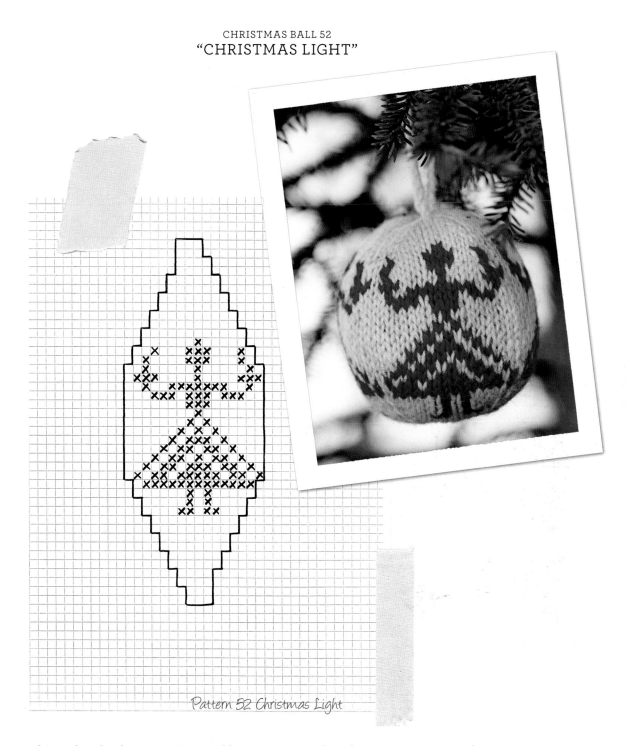

Pattern 52 Christmas Light

This girl with a lamp was inspired by a woman we found on a mitten pattern from the Vestland Handcraft Association in Bergen, Norway. The motif also resembles our Swedish candle holder shaped like an angel. We found the candle holder at a market in Gothenburg, Sweden some time after we had drawn our own angel.

THIS YEAR we put lighted candles on the tree, unfortunately we didn't have enough candles for all the candle holders so we substituted an old Christmas card for the candle in this holder.

"LIGHT OF THE THREE HOLY KINGS"

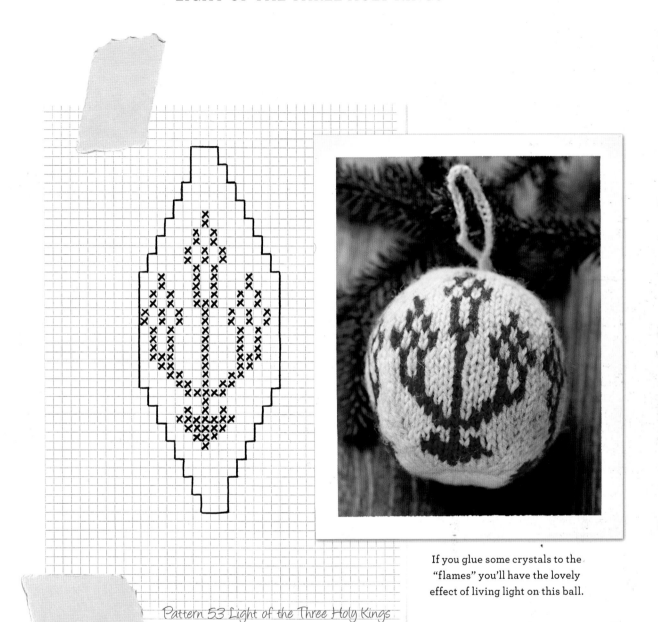

Pattern 53 Light of the Three Holy Kings

If you glue some crystals to the "flames" you'll have the lovely effect of living light on this ball.

6 of January, the thirteenth day of Christmas or Epiphany, is the day honoring the visit of the Three Holy Kings to the baby Jesus. In earlier times, this day was an even more important holiday than Christmas Eve. It was meant to be a day of rest and workmen were not supposed to labor in the forests that day. There are stories of people who worked on Epiphany with frightful consequences. One such person lost his reasoning after seeing a vision in the forest that day and he was never in his right mind again.

CHAPTER 18

A Christmas journey

WE DROVE to the farm in a horse-drawn sled. The snow lay heavily over the edges of the roof and was piled high on the sides of the road. Only a small strip of the logging road and some little windows could be glimpsed through the darkness. We tied up the horses in the barn and gave them some hay before we went into the warm house to visit the old people who lived on the farm.

THE COTTAGE was dark and low under the roof. It was warm and cozy and the old woman had long ago set out the seven kinds of cookies. Wide floorboards stretched out towards the old wood stove, before ending at a streaked hayrick. The old woman heated up the coffee and talked about life, wondering what was going on at our home and what the news from town was. Then we turned our eyes to the darkness and saw, above her head, a troll woman swaying on a broomstick. She was black-clad and gloomy and there was no doubt about who she was. It was the Thirteenth-Kari dancing above the warmth of the oven with her Kari-folk.

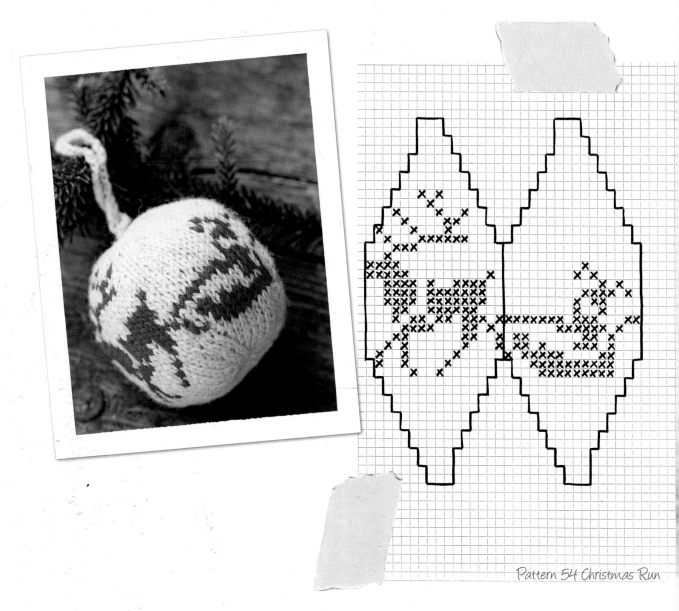

Pattern 54 Christmas Run

The pattern with the little man driving the sleigh with reindeer was drawn freestyle based on a picture we found in Annemor Sundbø's book, *Everyday Knitting*. This ball has a two-part pattern so we have two pictures. That way it's easier to see how the motif will look on the finished ball.

To "drive the Christmas Run" means to go on a Christmas visit. Some people go in sleighs and some drive other vehicles. At Carlos' great grandparents' place in Sweden, the Karlsson family used to drive a wagon with several black horses for their Christmas visits. If anyone wants to knit a car on their ornament, there's a blank piece of graph paper at the back of the book for you to chart it out. Good luck!

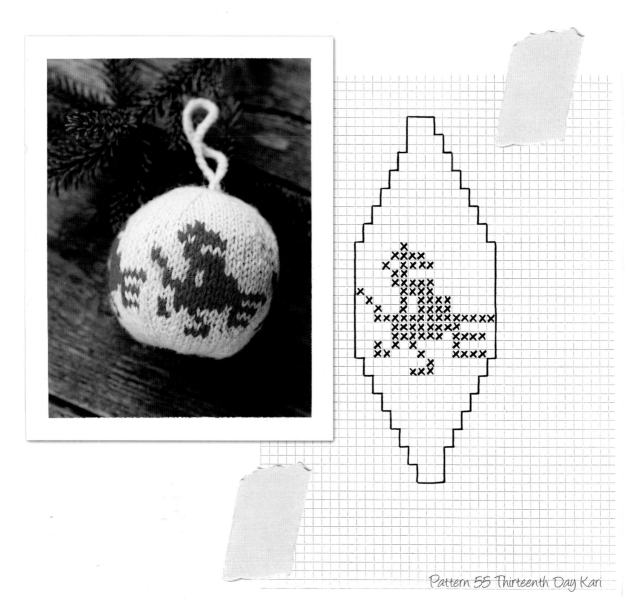

Pattern 55 Thirteenth Day Kari

"Can you tell me what the Thirteenth-Kari is? It is a witch or troll whom they believed couldn't mingle in the same society as Christians but was only allowed to come out once a year to make the Christmas run through the town and that was on the thirteenth night."

Quotation from Sidsel Sidserk by Hans Aanrud

Maybe it's a little unusual to have a Christmas ornament with a witch on it. Witches are usually associated with Easter in Sweden. But now almost everyone knows who Thirteenth-Kari is and so she has a place in our Christmas ball collection.

CHAPTER 19

Conclusion – the twelfth day

I crack a nutshell,
I long for some candy brittle
But everything is finished; It's Knut's Day,
And everything must be cleared out!

Good-bye, my beautiful star,
Good-bye my pixie friend!
Good-bye to all the ornaments – until next Christmas
We'll certainly meet again!

THE TWELFTH DAY – Britt G. Hallqvist

FACTS ABOUT TWELFTH DAY KNUT:

Knut Lavran was a Danish duke who was killed by his cousin and rival on January 7, 1131. Knut became a saint and Knut's Day which was originally January 7 but, in 1680, it was moved to January 13, 20 days after Christmas.

Merry Christmas!

BIBLIOGRAPHY

Børretzen, Odd. *Det norske folks bedrøvelige liv og historia [The Sad Life and History of the Norwegian People]*. Tiden Norsk Forlag, 1968.

McGregor, Sheila. *Traditional Scandinavian Knitting*. Mineola, New York: Dover, 1984

Norbury, James. *Traditional Knitting Patterns from Scandinavia, the British Isles, France, Italy and other European Countries*. New York: Dover, 1973.

Sibbern Bøhn, Annichen. *Norwegian Knitting Designs*. Oslo, Norway: Grøndahl & Søn, 1975.

Sundbø, Annemor. *Everyday Knitting: Treasures from a Ragpile*. Kristiansand, Norway; Torridal Tweed, 2000.

Invisible Threads in Knitting. Kristiansand, Norway; Torridal Tweed, 2007.

Upitis, Lizbeth. *Latvian Mittens* (revised edition). Pittsville, Wisconsin: Schoolhouse, 1997.

Aanrud, Hans, Sidsel Sidserk. The Norwegian Book Club, 1976.

Arne Nerjordet and Carlos Zachrison, Norwegian and Swedish respectively, established their design company ARNE & CARLOS in 2002. Drawing on their traditional Scandinavian influences and their natural environment, they create original and visually striking knitwear, and work with such prestigious international fashion designers as Comme des Garçons.

Arne and Carlos' creative base is their eclectic farm located north of Oslo in the Valdres region of Norway. There, they absorb the rich tradition of Scandinavian arts and crafts while exploring their own knitwear inspirations

Please visit their website for more inspiration, the latest news and more about Arne & Carlos at www.arne-carlos.com.

The Christmas balls were knitted with Dale of Norway "Heilo" yarn.
Weight: Sport/Double Knitting
Dale of Norway "Heilo" (100% wool, 109 yds/100 m, 50 g)

Arne and Carlos would like to thank everyone who has worked with them and who has contributed to making this book possible.
Many, many thanks!

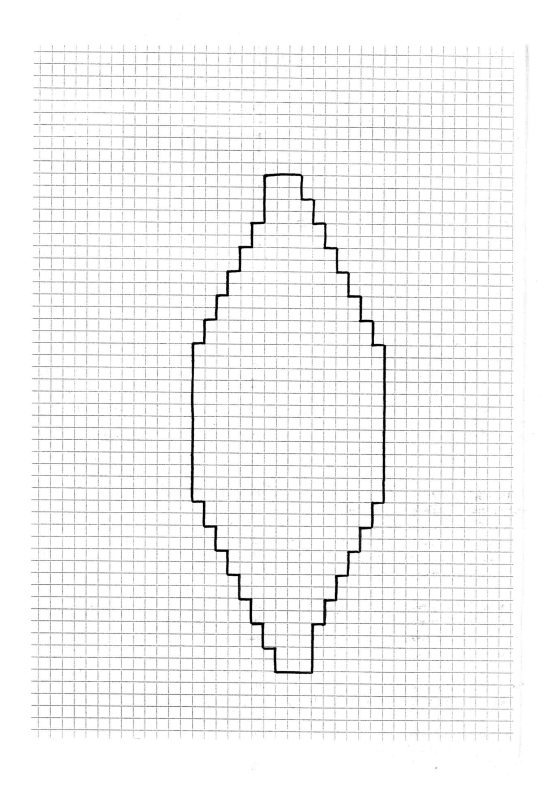

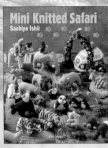